Singing
ENGLISH

22 PHOTOCOPIABLE SONGS AND CHANTS FOR LEARNING ENGLISH

HELEN MACGREGOR &
STEPHEN CHADWICK

Contents

Use the link below to access the audio:

www.collins.co.uk/singingenglish/download

Published by Collins
An imprint of HarperCollins*Publishers* Ltd
The News Building
1 London Bridge Street
London
SE1 9GF

HarperCollins*Publishers*
Macken House
39/40 Mayor Street Upper
Dublin 1, D01 C9W8
Ireland

www.collins.co.uk

Copyright © Helen MacGregor and Stephen Chadwick 2005
Audio © HarperCollins*Publishers* Ltd 2005
ISBN: 978-0-7136-7361-6

Edited by Lucy Poddington and Emily Wilson
Designed by Jocelyn Lucas
Cover illustration © Emma Harding 2005
Inside illustrations © Joy Gosney 2005
Audio produced by Stephen Chadwick at 3D Music Ltd Performed by
Kim Chandler and Chris Madin
Music set by Jeanne Roberts

A CIP catalogue record for this book is available from the British Library.

Introduction

Singing English is an exciting new collection of songs and chants which supports the teaching of English to beginners. It is intended for teachers and parents working with children who are learning English as a foreign or additional language.

The download comprises performance tracks sung by native English speakers and backing tracks for every song. The book contains photocopiable song words for each song and teaching ideas which develop children's abilities to communicate in English and to appreciate British culture. No music reading is required to use the resource. However, melody lines are provided at the back of the book for music readers.

The resource can be used alongside any scheme of work, or to help prepare for the Cambridge Young Learners English Tests run by University of Cambridge ESOL (English for Speakers of Other Languages) Examinations.

The songs, chants and activity ideas in **Singing English** help children to:

- enjoy and become familiar with the sounds of the English language;

- develop language skills and language-learning skills;

- become confident in speaking, understanding and reading a new language;

- learn about British culture and people.

Using the songs and chants

The songs and chants can be taught in any order to complement your teaching, but are arranged progressively in the book, with the later songs building on vocabulary already learnt and containing less repetition of words and phrases.

To familiarise children with the sounds of the English language and to develop good listening and aural memory skills, it is generally advisable to teach the songs using the audio or by singing them yourself before introducing the children to the written words. Singing the songs without the support of the audio enables you to adapt the pitch and tempo of each song to suit the particular needs of your children. It is important to revisit the songs with sufficient frequency over a period of time for the children to become confident with the language.

The track numbers are referred to at appropriate points throughout the teaching notes and a full track list can be found on page 64. You will be able to play the audio through a computer.

Guidance is given for each of the songs and chants about possible ways of teaching and performing them, for example:

- by joining in with key phrases or the chorus on first listening, then gradually learning the whole song;

- by performing in two groups;

- by inviting smaller groups or soloists to perform parts.

The resource is designed to be used flexibly so that you can adapt the songs and activities to cater for the age, ability and experience of the children.

Once the songs have been learnt, they can be sung regularly at any time, either with the backing track or unaccompanied. Many songs lend themselves to adding actions, dance steps and/or percussion accompaniments, and could be incorporated into music lessons. There are many opportunities suggested in the teaching notes for the children to develop the songs by writing their own verses. Performances could be recorded for discussion and evaluation.

Use the link below to access the audio:

www.collins.co.uk/singingenglish/download

Developing the vocabulary

For each song or chant, ideas are provided of ways to extend learning using the song vocabulary as a starting point. These activities may be completed at the same time as learning the song or may be used at a later stage. Often the children are asked to compose their own song words to perform with the backing track, offering opportunities for differentiation and independent learning.

Key vocabulary for each song is given in the key vocabulary box. Words and phrases which feature in the vocabulary lists for the Cambridge Young Learners English Tests are included here. The children could be encouraged to research further vocabulary using dictionaries.

Key to abbreviations used in vocabulary lists:	
adj	adjective
adv	adverb
conj	conjunction
det	determiner
int	interrogative
inter	interjection
n	noun
prep	preposition
pron	pronoun
v	verb

Follow-up work

Linked to each song or chant are suggestions for games, role plays, research projects and cross-curricular activities to further the children's knowledge of English language and British culture. These activities often involve combining vocabulary from a range of topics.

Many of the follow-up ideas can be used as extension activities for the more confident pupils, either working individually or in small groups. Other suggestions are suitable for use with the whole class, perhaps at a later stage, to consolidate and extend their learning. The activities incorporate reading, writing and use of ICT, and make other cross-curricular links with subjects such as maths and geography.

Photocopiable song words

When the children are able to sing a song confidently (or at a later stage), you can introduce them to the written song words on the photocopiable song sheets. These can be used in a variety of ways to support the development of literacy in the language. For example, the sheet could be:

- displayed as a song sheet on an OHT or interactive whiteboard;

- enlarged and displayed on the classroom wall as a poster;

- used in a lesson focusing on reading and writing;

- presented as a stimulus for composing new song words.

Resources

Few additional resources are required in order to learn the songs and use the teaching ideas. Number lines and a map of the UK will be useful, and occasionally other ideas for visual aids are suggested in the teaching notes. Many of the illustrations on the photocopiable song sheets can be enlarged for display. **Please note that any material not marked 'photocopiable' may not be photocopied.**

When using the suggestions for developing the vocabulary and follow-up work, try to ensure that the children have access to English dictionaries so that they can look up additional vocabulary.

Once the songs have been learnt, they can easily be performed unaccompanied as well.

Melody lines

Melody lines are provided at the back of the book for music readers. Teachers or pupils may wish to play the melody lines on a piano, keyboard or other pitched instrument when composing new song words.

Hello

audio tracks   **1**   the song   **2**   backing track

Using the song

All listen to the song (track 1). Ask the children to identify any words they recognise, such as **Hello**. Teach the vocabulary either by listening to the song or by saying the words yourself for the children to copy. Ensure that everyone knows the meaning of the words in each line, and explain that **I'm** is a short form of **I am**.

Learn to sing one line of the song at a time. When the class is familiar with the whole song, divide into two groups to sing the questions and answers (as demonstrated by the female and male singers). All join in with the last two lines of each verse.

When everyone is confident, sing the song in two parts with the backing track (track 2).

key vocabulary

day n	you pron
night n	bye inter
beautiful adj	goodbye inter
fine adj	good morning/
am v	afternoon/
are v	evening/night inter
a det	
how adv	hello inter thank
I pron	you inter

Developing the vocabulary

Using the backing track (track 2), sing the part of the leader (lines one and three), inserting the names of individual children. The individuals respond by singing the answer and your name, eg

Hello, Michelle! How are you?
Hello, Mrs Khan! I'm fine, thank you.

The whole class joins in with the last two lines of each verse.

In pairs, the children can then practise singing the questions and answers, taking it in turns to lead.

Introduce other ways of responding to the question **How are you?**, eg
I'm all right, thanks.
I'm OK.
I'm not very well.
Excellent, thanks.

Ask individuals the question for them to speak a reply.

Follow-up work

Introduce the class to the written words using the photocopiable song sheet. You could write other phrases on the board, eg **Great! We're fine. So am I. What did you say?**

Make sets of cards showing one greeting or phrase on each card. In small groups, the children choose cards and act out a scene using them, eg two children approach two others and call out greetings:

Child 1: **Hello, Sujata! Hi, Ivan!**
Child 2: **How are you?**
The others respond, eg
Child 3: **Hello, I'm fine!**
Child 4: **So am I!**

Each group performs their scene to the rest of the class.

Hello

Hello! Hello! How are you?

Hello! Hello! I'm fine, thank you.

Good morning! Good morning! How are you?

Good morning! Good morning! I'm fine, thank you.

Hello! Hello! Hi!

What a beautiful day!

Hello! Hello! How are you?

Hello! Hello! I'm fine, thank you.

Good afternoon! Good evening! Goodnight! Goodbye!

Good afternoon! Good evening! Goodnight! Goodbye!

Goodbye! Goodbye! Bye!

What a beautiful night!

The human body

audio tracks **3** the song **4** backing track

Using the song

Introduce the names of the parts of the body featured in the song. Before you begin teaching the song, ask the class to stand up so they can perform the actions. Listen to the song (track 3) and demonstrate appropriate actions as the words are sung, asking the class to copy you, eg

verse 1 – wink right eye, wink left eye, tap ears, touch nose;

verse 2 – raise right arm, raise left arm, clap hands, touch nose;

verse 3 – shake right leg, shake left leg, jump, touch nose.

When the children have learnt these actions, teach them actions for:

From the top of the head
Down to the toes

(eg touch top of head, then touch toes)

Learn to sing the song with track 3. Point out that the melody at the end of verse 2 is different from the end of verse 1. Practise both of these variations, then divide the class into two groups and try singing them together in two parts for verse 3.

When the class is familiar with the whole song, sing it with the backing track (track 4), dividing into two groups at the end of the last verse to sing the two-part melody.

key vocabulary

arm n	**nose** n
body n	**part** n
ear n	**the** det
eye n	**down** prep
foot/feet n	**from** prep
hand n	**of** prep
head n	**to** prep
leg n	**and** conj

Developing the vocabulary

Introduce vocabulary for other parts of the body, eg

back	**hip**
chin	**knee**
elbow	**neck**
face	**stomach**
hair	**tooth/teeth**

Encourage groups of children to devise and practise a new verse with actions, to perform to the class, eg

Hip, hip, knees and nose,
From the top of the head
Down to the toes ...

Follow-up work

When the children are familiar with positional and instructional vocabulary, play **Simon says**. Lead the game yourself at first; ask the children to perform an action, starting with the words **Simon says**, eg

Simon says, 'Put your hand on your head'.
Simon says, 'Clap your hands'.

The class must follow the instructions as long as they hear the words **Simon says**. If these words are omitted, eg **Stop clapping!**, the children must ignore the instruction. When children make a mistake they are 'out' of the game.

Individuals may take turns to lead the game.

The human body

Eye, eye, ears and nose,
From the top of the head
Down to the toes,
Eye, eye, ears and nose,
Parts of the human body.
Eye, eye, ears and nose.

Arm, arm, hands and nose,
From the top of the head
Down to the toes,
Arm, arm, hands and nose,
Parts of the human body.
Arm, arm, hands and nose,
Hands and nose.

Leg, leg, feet and nose,
From the top of the head
Down to the toes,
Leg, leg, feet and nose,
Parts of the human body.

☺ **Leg, leg,**   ☺ **Leg, leg, feet and nose,**
Feet and nose.   **Feet and nose.**
Feet and nose.   **Feet and nose.**

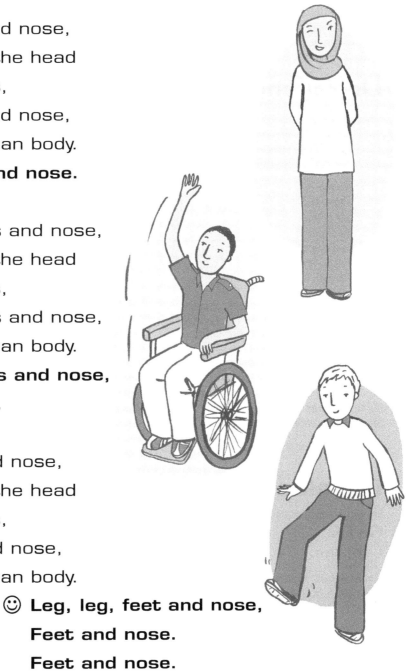

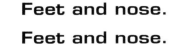

SINGING ENGLISH © HELEN MACGREGOR & STEPHEN CHADWICK 2005, HarperCollins*Publishers* Ltd

One to ten and back again

Using the song

Make a number line from one to ten and display it at the front of the class. Listen to the first half of the song (track 5), pointing to each number on the number line as it occurs.

Listen to the first half of the song again, and join in with the echo-chanting: listen to the numbers chanted by the singer and join in with the chanted echo. Repeat several times until everyone is confident with counting from one to ten. Then listen to the whole song, joining in with the echo-chanting.

Introduce zero, adding a number card for zero in the appropriate place on the number line. Learn to sing the melody of the song.

When everyone is confident, perform the whole song with the backing track (track 6). All sing the melody, then divide into two groups to echo-chant the numbers. Swap parts so that each group has an opportunity to lead the chant. Select an individual to point to the numbers on the number line as the class sings the song.

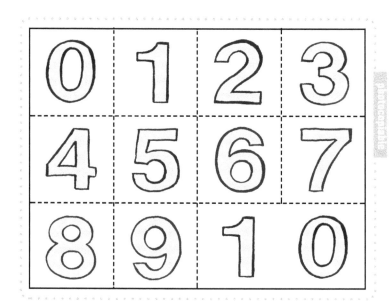

Developing the vocabulary

Introduce the question **How old are you?** and possible responses, eg

I'm ten.   **I'm ten years old.**
I am ten.   **I am ten years old.**

Make sets of number cards from one to ten. Give pairs of children a set of the cards each. Ask them to shuffle the cards and place them face down on the table. Explain that the card they turn over will show their pretend age. The children take turns to ask each other how old they are, eg

Child 1: **How old are you?**

Child 2 turns over card 6: **I'm six years old. How old are you?**

Child 1 turns over card 9: **I'm nine.**

Follow-up work

Make a set of number cards from zero to ten. Select eleven children to stand in a line facing the class and allocate a number card to each child, which they hold up for the class to see.

Invite an individual to put the children into a different order to make a new number sequence, eg

0 10 1 9 2 8 3 7 4 6 5

As the individual points to each card in turn, the class chants the new number sequence. Repeat the activity to give others a turn at composing number sequences.

To familiarise the class with the written number words, write the word on the back of each card and repeat the activity using the numbers in words instead of figures.

One to ten and back again

Get ready! Count to ten,
Up to ten, then back again.

One two three four five,
One two three four five,
Six seven eight nine ten.
Six seven eight nine ten.
One two three four five six seven
Eight nine ten.
One two three four five six seven
Eight nine ten.

Get ready! Count to ten,
Up to ten, then back again.

Ten nine eight seven six,
Ten nine eight seven six,
Five four three two one.
Five four three two one.
Ten nine eight seven six five four
Three two one.
Ten nine eight seven six five four
Three two one.

Count up high, count down low,
And don't forget zero!
(Zero! Zero! Zero! Zero! Zero!)

My favourite food

audio tracks   **7** the song   **8** backing track

Using the song

Listen to the song (track 7) and all join in with the chorus. Ensure that the children understand the meaning of the words in the chorus, and point out that **what's** is a short form of **what is**. Ask the children if they recognise any of the foods in the verses. Discuss that the foods in each verse begin with the same letter (alliteration).

Teach the verses one at a time, either by listening to the song or by saying the words yourself for the children to copy. You could use an enlarged photocopy of the song sheet to help with the meaning of the words.

When everyone is confident, sing the whole song with the backing track (track 8).

Developing the vocabulary

Introduce more food vocabulary, eg

apple	**orange**
banana	**potato**
cheese	**rice**
chicken	**salad**
egg	**soup**
fish	**spaghetti**
ice cream	**tomato**

As a class, make up new verses for the song (the words for the foods do not need to start with the same letter). All sing the new verses with the backing track (track 8).

Invite three small groups or individuals to make up a new verse each. The class sings the chorus and each group or soloist sings their verse in between. The class can join in with **Oh yeah!** each time it is sung.

key vocabulary

bean n	**favourite** adj
bread n	**is** v
burger n	**like** v
cake n	**my** det
carrot n	**your** det
coconut n	**I** pron
food n	**that** pron
pea n	**and** conj
pear n	**what** int
pineapple n	

Follow-up work

Teach the class the phrases **I don't like ...** and **That's not my favourite food.**

As a class, use these phrases to make up new verses about foods the children do not like, eg

I don't like tomatoes,
Oh no! I don't like tomatoes,
That's not my favourite food.

All sing the new verses with the backing track (track 8).

When the class is confident with the new phrases, encourage small groups or individuals to make up their own verses of the song, including both their likes and dislikes.

My favourite food

Oh, what's your favourite food?
What's your favourite food?
Oh, munch, munch, crunch, crunch,
What's your favourite food?

Beans, bread and burgers,
Oh yeah! I like beans, bread and burgers,
That's my favourite food.

Oh, what's your favourite food ...

Coconuts, cake and carrots,
Oh yeah! I like coconuts, cake and carrots,
That's my favourite food.

Oh, what's your favourite food ...

Pineapple, peas and pears,
Oh yeah! I like pineapple, peas and pears,
That's my favourite food.

Oh, what's your favourite food ...

SINGING ENGLISH © HELEN MACGREGOR & STEPHEN CHADWICK 2005, HarperCollins*Publishers* Ltd

The alphabet

audio tracks   **9**   the song   **10**   backing track

Using the song

Show the class an enlarged copy of the alphabet on the photocopiable song sheet.

Listen to the song (track 9), pointing to each letter in turn to familiarise the class with the letter names. All practise the pronunciation, either using the song or by saying the letters one by one for the children to copy. Then all join in singing the letter names in the song.

Practise singing the song with track 9 and ensure that everyone understands the meaning of the key vocabulary. When the class is familiar with the whole song, sing it with the backing track (track 10). Invite individuals to conduct by pointing to the letters as they are sung.

Developing the vocabulary

Play **Hangman** with the class. Select a word from vocabulary already learnt, such as the name of a food. Mark on the board the numbers of letters the word contains, eg _ _ _ _ _ _ _ (**coconut**).

Going round the class in turn, invite individuals to suggest a letter name. If the letter is found in the word, write it in the appropriate space (or spaces); if not, write the letter elsewhere on the board, as a reminder of which letters have been suggested. The first child to correctly identify the word may choose the next word to lead the game.

key vocabulary

alphabet n	will v
head n	the det
easy adj	your det
is v	at prep
learn v	to prep
say v	with prep
see v	me pron
start v	you pron
stay v	and conj
use v	

Follow-up work

Introduce or revise the following phrases:

What is your name?

My name is ...

Teach the question **How do you spell that?** Give the children the opportunity to practise spelling their names. Some may be able to spell both first name and surname.

Make several name cards, eg **Jane, Kim, Sita, John, Paul, Raj**. Give the cards to individuals, who take turns to spell out the name on the card as the class writes down the letters. All practise the pronunciation of the names and compare the written answers with the cards to check spellings.

The alphabet

Say the alphabet with me,

A B C D

Keep to the beat and you will see,

A B C D E F G

Learning the alphabet is easy!

A B C D E F G

H I J K L M N O P

Stay cool and use your head,

You start at A and end at Z!

A B C D E F G

H I J K L M N O P

Q R S T U V W

X Y Z

SINGING ENGLISH © HELEN MACGREGOR & STEPHEN CHADWICK 2005, HarperCollinsPublishers Ltd

I like swimming

sports and leisure-time activities

audio tracks **11** the song **12** backing track

Using the song

Listen to the song (track 11) several times, then all join in singing the phrases **Yes, I like swimming/reading/singing.**

Teach the rest of the vocabulary either using the song or by saying the words yourself for the children to copy.

Once the class is familiar with the song, divide into two groups to match the female and male voices. Group one begins and group two sings the questions, then group one sings the replies. The groups swap parts for the second verse, and swap back again for the third verse. When everyone is confident, sing the song with the backing track (track 12).

Developing the vocabulary

Make a list on the board of the children's favourite sports and hobbies, extending the vocabulary as required, eg

playing … (badminton, basketball, cricket, football, the guitar, the piano, tennis, rugby)
dancing
fishing
listening to music
painting
watching television/TV

Introduce the phrases **I love**, **I don't mind**, **I prefer**, **I don't like** and **I hate**. In pairs, the children discuss the sports and activities they like best and those they do not like, eg

Do you like playing cricket?
No, I prefer playing tennis.

Invite pairs to prepare and practise a new verse to sing to the class, eg

I don't like football! But I love fishing!
After school, at weekends, every day,
I love fishing!
Do you like fishing?
Yes, I like fishing …

key vocabulary

day n	swim v
school n	every det
weekend n	after prep
do v	at prep
like v	I pron
read v	you pron
sing v	yes inter

Follow-up work

Carry out a class survey to find out how many children like each of the sports and activities. As a class, make a bar chart of the most and least popular.

Make a class sports and hobbies magazine. Begin by looking at magazines and/or the internet to find pictures of British sports and hobbies. Working in groups, the children produce pictures and captions for the class magazine, using ICT if possible.

Encourage the children to use dictionaries to look up other vocabulary they may need, eg

a team, a tennis player, the captain, the World Cup, the Olympics, a competition, the winner, to win, to lose

As a class, choose a title for the magazine.

I like swimming

I like swimming! I like swimming!

After school, at weekends, every day,

I like swimming!

Do you like swimming?

Yes, I like swimming.

Do you like swimming?

Yes, I like swimming.

I like reading! I like reading!

After school, at weekends, every day,

I like reading!

Do you like reading?

Yes, I like reading.

Do you like reading?

Yes, I like reading.

I like singing! I like singing!

After school, at weekends, every day,

I like singing!

Do you like singing?

Yes, I like singing.

Do you like singing?

Yes, I like singing.

Singing!

My family

family, friends and ourselves

Using the song

Enlarge and cut out the individual pictures of family members on the photocopiable song sheet. Hold up the cards and introduce the class to the characters' names. Select four children to stand in a line facing the class, holding up the cards in the following order: **Dad, Mum, Katie, David**.

All listen to the song (track 13). Point to each card in turn as the words **father, mother, sister, brother** are sung, then as the characters' names are sung: **Mum and Dad, Katie, David**.

Teach the vocabulary in the first seven lines of the song, pointing out that **I'd like** is a short form of **I would like**. Then practise singing this part of the song.

When the children are confident, introduce the words for the other members of the family: **aunt/aunty, uncle, grandparents, Grandma, Grandad**. All listen to the parts of the song marked with an ear symbol on the photocopiable song sheet, joining in with the phrases **How do you do?** and **Let's all have some tea!** if you wish. Sing the song with track 13, then with the backing track (track 14).

key vocabulary

aunt n	are v
baby n	is v
brother n	meet v
dad n	would like v
family n	all det
father n	my det
grandparent n	I pron
mother n	these pron
mum n	this pron
parent n	you pron
sister n	and conj
uncle n	

Developing the vocabulary

As a class, practise alternative ways of introducing friends or family, eg **I'd like to introduce you to ...**

Teach additional vocabulary for family members, eg

daughter	**stepfather**
son	**stepmother**
grandfather	**stepbrother**
grandmother	**stepsister**
grandson	**cousin**
granddaughter	

In groups, the children make up a family for role play, deciding on names and the relationships in the family. Invite children to introduce themselves and the other members of their group to the class, eg

I am Sam. This is my father. This is my sister, Sally, and this is my cousin, John.

Follow-up work

Ask the children to draw portraits or bring in photos of people in their own families. Each child prepares a presentation for the class using vocabulary already learnt, eg

My name is Anisha. I live in Leeds. These are my parents. This is my sister, Nishma, and this is my baby brother, Anil. He's one year old.

Introduce further vocabulary, eg

This is my elder brother/sister. He/She is the eldest.
This is my younger brother/sister. He/She is the youngest.

My family

I'd like you to meet all my family,
Father, mother, sister, brother,
Meet my family, meet my family.

These are my parents, Mum and Dad,
This is my sister, Katie,
This is my baby brother, David,
This is my family, this is my family.

Now you've said '**How do you do?**' to my family,
Come inside and make yourself at home!
Let's all have some tea!

I'd like you to meet all my family,
Aunt, uncle, grandparents,
Meet my family, meet my family.

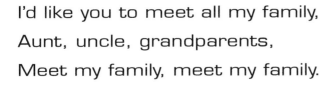

This is my Aunty Emily,
This is my Uncle Michael,
This is my Grandma and my Grandad,
This is my family, this is my family.

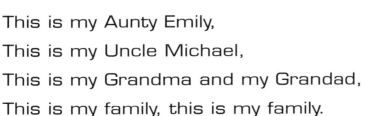

Now you've said '**How do you do?**' to my family ...

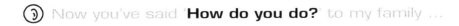

Let's all have some tea!

My house

Using the song

Enlarge and display the pictures on the photocopiable song sheet. All listen to the song (track 15). Point to the animals as their names are sung. As the list of animals grows verse by verse, encourage the children to join in.

Teach the chorus either by listening to the song or by saying the words yourself for the children to copy. Then teach the vocabulary for each verse, pointing out how the words begin with the same sounds (eg **goat** and **garden**) and how phrases are added and repeated as the list of animals grows.

When the children are confident with the whole song, sing it with the backing track (track 16).

Developing the vocabulary

Teach vocabulary for more animals, eg

cat	**frog**	**sheep**
cow	**horse**	**snake**
dog	**monkey**	**spider**
duck	**mouse**	**whale**

Also introduce vocabulary for more rooms and furniture in the house, eg

bedroom	**armchair**	**table**
dining room	**cupboard**	**television/TV**
hall	**sofa**	**window**

Introduce more prepositions, eg

behind	**on**
next to	**under**

In small groups, the children make up a line for a new version of the song, eg **There's a dog on the sofa.** They may wish to draw a picture as a reminder of the meaning of the words. Sing the new verses with the backing track (track 16).

key vocabulary

bat n	will v
bathroom n	a det
crocodile n	all det
friend n	my det
garden n	the det
goat n	there adv
house n	too adv
kitchen n	at prep
living room n	in prep
lizard n	to prep
party n	with prep
are v	me pron
be v	there pron
come v	we pron
have v	you pron
is v	when conj
stay v	

Follow-up work

Ask the children to draw a picture of a house, choosing one animal for each room and placing it wherever they like in the room (the words do not have to start with the same sounds). Invite the children to show the class their drawings and to talk about where the animals are, eg

There's a dog in the dining room, a duck on the TV, a sheep in the shower and a spider under the sofa.

The children could work in small groups to make up a new version of the song based on some of their drawings. Encourage them to practise singing their song before performing it to the class.

My house

When you come to stay with me,
We will have a party!
All my friends will be there too,
When you stay at my house.
There's a goat in the garden.

When you come to stay with me ...
There's a crocodile in the kitchen
And a goat in the garden.

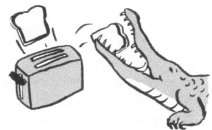

When you come to stay with me ...
There's a lizard in the living room,
A crocodile in the kitchen
And a goat in the garden.

When you come to stay with me ...
There's a bat in the bathroom,
A lizard in the living room,
A crocodile in the kitchen
And a goat in the garden.

All my friends are in the house,
All my friends are in the house!

photocopiable

Ten to one hundred

audio tracks   **17** the chant   **18** backing track

Using the song

Make two number lines, one showing all the numbers from ten to twenty and another showing the multiples of ten from twenty to one hundred (ie **20**, **30**, **40** ...). Display the number lines at the front of the class.

Listen to the first verse of the song (track 17) with the class and point to each number on the number line as it occurs in the song. Teach the numbers ten to twenty either by listening to the song or by saying the numbers yourself for the children to copy. Then all join in echo-singing this verse: listen to the numbers sung by the female singer and join in with the echo (male singer).

Pause the track at the end of the first verse and teach the class the multiples of ten from twenty to one hundred by saying the numbers yourself for the children to copy. Then all join in echo-singing the rest of the song.

When everyone is confident, divide into two groups to echo-sing the song with the backing track (track 18). Swap parts so that each group has an opportunity to lead the song.

key vocabulary

ten – 10	thirty – 30
eleven – 11	forty – 40
twelve – 12	fifty – 50
thirteen – 13	sixty – 60
fourteen – 14	seventy – 70
fifteen – 15	eighty – 80
sixteen – 16	ninety – 90
seventeen – 17	one hundred – 100
eighteen – 18	in prep
nineteen – 19	to prep
twenty – 20	

Developing the vocabulary

All sit in a circle. Take turns to chant a number, starting at ten and finishing at twenty. Repeat several times around the circle, then include all the numbers from one to twenty.

Play **Number shuffle**. Make a set of number cards from one to twenty. Shuffle the cards, then hold them up one by one for the class or individuals to say the numbers. Repeat using the multiples of ten from twenty to one hundred.

Play **Bingo** with the class. Each child draws a grid of twelve squares and writes in any twelve numbers between one and twenty. Shuffle a set of number cards from one to twenty, then call out numbers one at a time. When the children hear a number they have written down, they cross it off their grid. The first child to cross off all twelve numbers shouts **Bingo** and wins the game. The winner may become the next caller when you play the game again.

Follow-up work

Teach the class the phrase **How many is that?** Play mental maths games using number cards from one to twenty. Select two cards and hold them up for the class to see. Ask addition questions, eg

I have six and ten. How many is that?

Make addition sums with answers above twenty and ask if anyone can work out how to say the answer, eg **twenty-five**.

Play the game again using two sets of number cards from ten to twenty, to make additions with answers from twenty to forty.

To familiarise the class with the written number words, make cards which show the numbers in words and ask individuals or groups to match the numbers in words with the numbers in figures.

Ten to one hundred

Ten, eleven, twelve, thirteen,
Fourteen, fifteen.
Ten, eleven, twelve, thirteen,
Fourteen, fifteen.
Sixteen, seventeen,
Eighteen, nineteen, twenty.
Sixteen, seventeen,

Eighteen, nineteen, twenty.

Carry on in tens,
Twenty, thirty, forty, fifty.
Carry on in tens,
Twenty, thirty, forty, fifty.
Sixty, seventy,
Eighty, ninety, one hundred.
Sixty, seventy,
Eighty, ninety, one hundred.

Ten to one hundred.
Ten to one hundred.

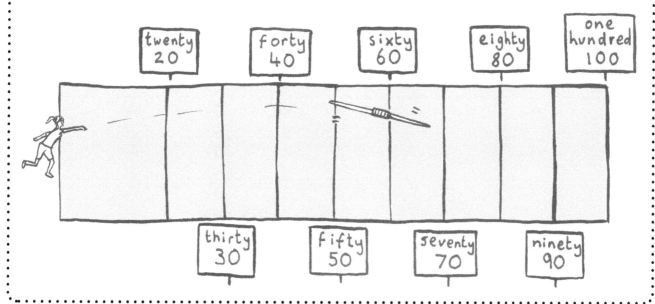

photocopiable

Are you hungry?

food and drink/requests

audio tracks   **19**   the chant   **20**   backing track

Using the song

First teach the children the phrases **It's time for breakfast/ lunch/ dinner** by saying them for the children to copy. Listen to the song (track 19) and all join in with the first line of each verse.

Teach the phrases in the second line of each verse and ensure the children understand their meanings. Listen to the song again, and join in with the first two lines of each verse. Ask the class if they can identify any of the foods in the song. Then teach the rest of the song. Remind the children that **it's** is a short form of **it is**, **I'd like** is a short form of **I would like**, and so on. Sing the whole song with track 19.

Once the class is familiar with the song, divide into two groups to match the male and female voices. Group one sings the first two lines, and group two sings the rest of the verse. The groups swap parts for the second verse, and swap back again for the third verse. When everyone is confident, sing the song with the backing track (track 20).

Developing the vocabulary

Introduce or revise other food and drink vocabulary, eg

apple	coffee	hot chocolate
banana	cup (of)	lemonade
biscuit	curry	pizza
chapati	fish	sandwich
cheese	French fries	tea
chocolate	fruit	toast

Use pictures of food (cut out of magazines or from food packaging) to help with the meanings.

As a class, compose three new verses for the song, eg

For breakfast I'd like some eggs and toast,
Please may I have some eggs and toast?
An apple and some hot chocolate,
Thank you very much, that's enough for me!

Sing the new version of the song with the backing track (track 20).

key vocabulary

bowl (of) n	are v
bread n	eat v
breakfast n	have v
chicken n	is v
dinner n	may v
egg n	would like v
glass (of) n	a det
jam n	some det
juice n	for prep
lunch n	enough pron
mango n	I pron
milk n	it pron
orange n	me pron
pasta n	that pron
rice n	you pron
soup n	and conj
time n	what int
tomato n	please inter
hungry adj	thank you very much inter

Follow-up work

Provide food packaging for the class to investigate more vocabulary for food and ingredients.

Play **In the café**. In small groups, the children compile and design café menus using the food and drink vocabulary they have learnt. Practise the following phrases with the class:

What would you like to eat?
Anything else?

In their groups, the children take it in turns to play the role of waiter/waitress and customers. Each waiter/ waitress invites individuals to order food and drink from the menus, writing down the orders if desired.

When numbers up to one hundred have been learnt, prices can be added to the menus. The waiters/ waitresses can then work out the customers' bills and ask for payment.

Are you hungry?

It's time for breakfast, time for breakfast.
What would you like to eat? Are you hungry?
For breakfast I'd like some bread and jam.
Please may I have some bread and jam?
A boiled egg and orange juice,
Thank you very much, that's enough for me!

It's time for lunch, time for lunch.
What would you like to eat? Are you hungry?
For lunch I'd like a bowl of soup.
Please may I have a bowl of soup?
Some pasta and tomato sauce,
Thank you very much, that's enough for me!

It's time for dinner, time for dinner.
What would you like to eat? Are you hungry?
For dinner I'd like some chicken and rice. Please
may I have some chicken and rice?
A mango and a glass of milk,
Thank you very much, that's enough for me!

photocopiable

Everyone is travelling

audio tracks   **21** the song   **22** backing track

Using the song

All listen to the song (track 21) and join in with the word **walk** each time it is repeated at the end of the verse. Then teach the class the chorus (**Travelling, travelling ...**), either by listening to the song or by saying the words yourself for the children to copy.

Show the class enlarged copies of the pictures on the photocopiable song sheet. Introduce the names of the different means of transport one at a time. Then teach the vocabulary for the rest of the verse. Point out that **isn't** is a short form of **is not**.

Sing the whole song with track 21, then with the backing track (track 22).

Developing the vocabulary

Ask the children to suggest other ways of travelling, eg **bicycle/**

bike	**motorbike**	**spaceship**
helicopter	**on foot**	**camel**
lorry	**taxi**	**horse**

Substitute other means of transport in the verse according to the children's suggestions, eg

We can travel in a spaceship,
Travel on a train,
On a horse, on a camel,
Or in a plane.

All sing the new version of the song with the backing track (track 22).

key vocabulary

boat n	the det
bus n	your det
car n	far adv
plane n	how adv
shoe n	not adv
train n	there adv
way n	too adv
world n	in prep
best adj	on prep
can v	everyone pron
get v	it pron
is v	we pron
put on v	and conj
walk v	but conj
will v	if conj
a det	or conj

Follow-up work

Teach the class the use of **by** with means of transport, eg **to travel by train**.

Carry out a class survey of the means of transport used to travel to school. Ask individuals around the class **How do you come to school?** The individuals reply giving the means of transport they use, eg

I come to school by bus and on foot.

Make a tally chart to record the number of children who use each means of transport. Draw a class bar chart on paper or on a computer and encourage the children to discuss the totals, eg

Eight children come to school by car.

Everyone is travelling

Travelling, travelling,
Travelling, oh yeah!
Everyone is travelling
All over the world.
Travelling, travelling,
Travelling, oh yeah!
How will we get there?
All over the world.

We can travel in a car,
Travel on a train,
On a bus, on a boat,
Or in a plane.
But the best way to travel,
If it isn't too far,
Is to put on your shoes
And walk, walk, walk, walk,
Put on your shoes and walk, walk, walk.

photocopiable

Weather report

audio tracks   **23** the song   **24** backing track

Using the song

Begin by teaching the children the names of the days of the week, either using the song (track 23) or by saying the words yourself for the children to copy. Explain to the class that the song describes the weather for each day of the week. Then listen to the song, all joining in with the first and last lines of each verse as they become familiar.

Photocopy and cut out these weather symbols. On the board, draw a chart with seven rows and two columns. Write the days of the week in the first column. All listen to one verse at a time. Ask the children to select the matching weather symbol and fix it to the chart next to the correct day.

Sing the whole song several times and repeat the weather chart activity until the children are confident with the vocabulary and matching the phrases with the symbols. Then sing the whole song with the backing track (track 24).

Developing the vocabulary

Display a large map of the UK. Introduce or revise the names of the parts of the UK: **England**, **Scotland**, **Wales** and **Northern Ireland**.

As a class, choose four weather symbols to fix to the map on England, Scotland, Wales and Northern Ireland. All chant the weather report you have created, eg

In England it is stormy.
In Scotland it is snowing.
In Wales it is sunny.
In Northern Ireland it is windy.
That's the weather today!

key vocabulary

fog n	dark adj
Friday n	dry adj
Monday n	foggy adj
morning n	hot adj
Saturday n	sunny adj
sky n	windy adj
snow n + v	wet adj
storm n	warm adj
Sunday n	is v
Thursday n	fall v
Tuesday n	rain v
wind n	the det
weather n	today adv
Wednesday n	like prep
blue adj	on prep
cloudy adj	it pron
cold adj	what int

Follow-up work

Play **Weather reporter** in small groups. Give each group two maps of the UK and two sets of the weather symbols above.

One child takes a map and, without showing the rest of the group, places four weather symbols on England, Scotland, Wales and Northern Ireland. The other children take turns to ask questions so that they can make a matching weather report on the second map, eg

Child 1: **Is it snowing anywhere?**

Weather reporter: **No, it isn't snowing anywhere.**

Child 2: **Is it sunny anywhere?**

Weather reporter: **Yes, it's sunny in Scotland.**

At the end, the children should compare maps to check that they match. Repeat the game so that each child has an opportunity to be the weather reporter.

Weather report

It's Monday morning, what's the weather like today? It's hot, it's dry – blue sky.
It's sunny weather on Monday, it's sunny today.

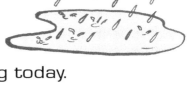

It's Tuesday morning ...
It's wet, it's cold – raindrops.
It's rainy weather on Tuesday, it's raining today.

It's Wednesday morning ...
It's dull, it's cool – wind blows.
It's windy weather on Wednesday,
it's windy today.

It's Thursday morning ...
It's cloudy, it's warm – thunderstorm.
It's stormy weather on Thursday,
it's stormy today.

It's Friday morning ...
It's dark, it's damp – thick fog.
It's foggy weather on Friday, it's foggy today.

It's Saturday morning ...
It's frosty, it's bright – snow falls.
It's snowy weather on Saturday,
it's snowing today.

It's Sunday morning ...
It's hot, it's dry – blue sky.
It's sunny weather on Sunday,
it's sunny today.

photocopiable

People all over the world

audio tracks   **25** the song   **26** backing track

Using the song

All listen to the song (track 25), then ask the children if they recognise any of the words or phrases.

Teach the verses one at a time, either by listening to the song or by saying the words yourself for the children to copy. Draw attention to the way the verb **to be** changes throughout the song. Also discuss that the adjectives in each verse have opposite meanings. Then all join in singing the verses with track 25.

Teach the chorus line by line, making sure that the children understand the meaning of the words. Point out that **we're** is a short form of **we are**. Sing the whole song with track 25, then with the backing track (track 26).

Developing the vocabulary

Introduce other pairs of adjectives with opposite meanings, eg

hot/cold
slow/fast
right/wrong
early/late

As a class, make up new verses using these adjectives. All sing the new version of the song with the backing track (track 26), eg

I am hot, you are cold,
He is hot, she is cold ...

Introduce the future (using **will**) and past simple forms of the verb **to be**:

I will be happy, you will be sad ...
I was happy, you were sad ...

Sing another new version of the song with the backing track, using either the future or the past simple forms as well as new adjectives.

key vocabulary

difference n	is v
person/people n	make v
	the det
place n	our det
world n	together adv
better adj	in prep
happy adj	all pron
old adj	I pron
sad adj	he pron
short adj	she pron
tall adj	they pron
young adj	we pron
am v	you pron
are v	and conj
can v	

Follow-up work

Revise other verbs, such as **to like**, **to play**, **to buy**. Practise conjugating them, eg

I like
you like
he/she likes
we like
you like
they like

Encourage pairs or individuals to make up new verses for the song, using vocabulary already learnt, eg

I like pasta, you like rice ...
I play tennis, you play golf ...

Invite the children to sing their new verses with the backing track (track 26).

People all over the world

I am happy, you are sad,
He is happy, she is sad,
We are happy, you are sad,
They are happy, they are sad.

People, people all over the world,
We're all in the human race.
Celebrate our differences
And together we can make our
world A better place.

I am young, you are old,
He is young, she is old,
We are young, you are old,
They are young, they are old.

People, people all over the world …

I am short, you are tall,
He is short, she is tall,
We are short, you are tall,
They are short, they are tall.

People, people all over the world …

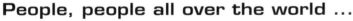

SINGING ENGLISH © HELEN MACGREGOR & STEPHEN CHADWICK 2005, HarperCollins*Publishers* Ltd

Going shopping

Using the song

All listen to the song (track 27), joining in with the chorus as it becomes familiar. Check that the children know that **we're** means **we are** and **let's** means **let us**.

Teach the class the vocabulary one verse at a time, either by listening to the song or by saying the phrases yourself for the children to copy. You could use an enlarged photocopy of the song sheet to help with the meaning of the words. Ensure the children know that British money is in pounds and pence, and check they know how this is written.

Sing the song with track 27, then with the backing track (track 28). If you wish, divide the class into two groups to sing the parts of customer and shop assistant. All sing the chorus. Swap parts so that everyone has a chance to practise each role.

Alternatively, a confident individual could sing the part of the shop assistant as a solo.

Developing the vocabulary

Introduce more shopping phrases, eg

How much does it cost?

It's too expensive.

I haven't got enough money.

Teach the children the names of other items they may wish to buy, holding up pictures or, if possible, actual objects, eg

comic	**drink**	**magazine**
mobile phone	**newspaper**	**postcard**
stamp	**watch**	

As a class, choose four items to include in a new version of the song. Make a price label for each item using numbers up to 100, and practise saying the prices.

Sing the new version of the song with the backing track (track 28). Hold up the items (or pictures of items) and the price labels as prompts at the appropriate moment.

key vocabulary

two – 2	**is** v
five – 5	**let's** v
nine – 9	**shall** v
twenty – 20	**the** det
forty-five – 45	**this** det
fifty – 50	**here** adv
ninety-nine – 99	**how much** adv
book n	**at** prep
camera n	**to** prep
CD n	**with** prep
football n	**me** pron
money n	**we** pron
shop n + v	**you** pron
are v	**what** int
buy v	**please** inter
come v	**thank you very**
go v	**much** inter

Follow-up work

Set up a shop in the classroom, using real objects or pictures of objects. Check that the children know the names of all the items.

Appoint two children as shop assistants. Ask them to decide on the prices of the items for sale and to make price labels. Then invite individuals to play the role of customers, using the shopping vocabulary and phrases they have learnt.

Once the children are familiar with the past tense, they could show their purchases to the class and describe what they bought, eg

Shopper: **I bought a postcard.**

Class: **How much was it?**

Shopper: **It was fifty pence.**

Going shopping

Come with me! We're going shopping.
Come with me! We're going to the shops.
Money, money, let's spend money.
What shall we buy?
What shall we buy at the shops?

'How much is this book, please?'
'Two pounds twenty.'
'Here you are. Thank you very much!'
'How much is this CD?'
'Nine pounds ninety-nine.'
'Thank you very much!'

Come with me! We're going shopping ...

'How much is this football?'
'Five pounds fifty.'
'Here you are. Thank you very much!'
'How much is this camera?'
'Twenty pounds forty-five.'
'Thank you very much!'

Come with me! We're going shopping ...

What shall we buy at the shops?

SINGING ENGLISH © HELEN MACGREGOR & STEPHEN CHADWICK 2005, HarperCollins*Publishers* Ltd

Happy birthday

audio tracks **29** the song **30** backing track

Using the song

All listen to the song (track 29). Teach the names of the months, either by listening to the song or by saying them yourself for the children to copy. Then explain that when the male singer chants the months, anyone with a birthday in the relevant month should raise their hand as the month is named. Listen to the song again so that the children can practise this.

Teach the vocabulary for the rest of the song, either by listening to the song or by saying it yourself for the children to copy. Practise singing the whole song with track 29, then perform it with the backing track (track 30).

Developing the vocabulary

Introduce the class to ordinal numbers from first to thirty-first:

first – 1st	**eleventh** – 11th	**twenty-first** – 21st
second – 2nd	**twelfth** – 12th	**twenty-second** – 22nd
third – 3rd	**thirteenth** – 13th	**thirtieth** – 30th
fourth – 4th	**fourteenth** – 14th	**thirty-first** – 31st
fifth – 5th	**fifteenth** – 15th	
sixth – 6th	**sixteenth** – 16th	
seventh – 7th	**seventeenth** – 17th	
eighth – 8th	**eighteenth** – 18th	
ninth – 9th	**nineteenth** – 19th	
tenth – 10th	**twentieth** – 20th	

Ask the children to work out how to say the day and month of their birthday, eg **My birthday is the first of February** (or **February the first**). Practise this by asking individuals **What date is your birthday?**

Teach the class additional useful vocabulary, eg

spring	**calendar**
summer	**Happy New Year**
autumn	**Happy Christmas**
winter	**Happy Easter**

key vocabulary

April n	happy adj
August n	come v
birthday n	is v
cake n	make v
December n	tell v
February n	a det
January n	the det
June n	your det
July n	on prep
March n	to prep
May n	it pron
month n	me pron
November n	you pron
October n	or conj
September n	when int
wish n	which int

Follow-up work

Divide the class into groups and give one group a blank calendar. Each child takes a turn to ask another group member when his or her birthday is, eg **Aisha, what date is your birthday?**

Aisha answers with the date of her birthday and the questioner writes her name on the relevant date on the calendar.

When the birthdays of everyone in the group are recorded on the calendar, it is passed in turn around the other groups. The completed calendar of class birthdays can be displayed in the classroom and used throughout the year to reinforce vocabulary.

Happy birthday

Happy birthday, happy birthday to you.
Happy birthday, happy birthday to you.
Congratulations! It's your birthday!
Happy birthday, happy birthday to you.
Blow out the candles on your cake,
Make a wish, hope it comes true.
Congratulations! It's your birthday!
Happy birthday, happy birthday to you.

When is your birthday?
Tell me which month –
January, February,
March, April or May,
June, July,
August, September,
October, November
Or December?

January	February
March	April
May	June
July	August
September	October
November	December

Happy birthday, happy birthday to you ...

What time is it?

asking the time/time expressions

audio tracks   **31** the song   **32** backing track

Using the song

Listen to the song (track 31) and all join in with the chorus and the **tick tock** lines as they become familiar. At the beginning of each verse, show the class a clock face set to the correct time. Ensure the children understand the meaning of the time vocabulary (**second, minute ...**) in the chorus.

Teach the verses one at a time, either by listening to the song or by saying the words yourself for the children to copy. You could use an enlarged photocopy of the song sheet to help the class remember some of the activities.

When everyone is confident, sing the whole song with track 31, then with the backing track (track 32).

Developing the vocabulary

Use a clock face to gradually introduce more time vocabulary, eg

half past	**twenty past/to**
quarter past/to	**twenty-five past/to**
five past/to	**midday/midnight**
ten past/to	

Also revise or introduce additional useful vocabulary, eg

evening	**breakfast**
a.m./p.m.	**lunch**
early/late	**tea**
bed	**dinner**
	supper

As a class, compose new verses for the song, choosing different times of day and appropriate activities, eg

It's quarter past nine in the evening,
Tick tock tick tock,
It's quarter past nine, it's time for bed.

Sing the new version of the song with the backing track (track 32).

key vocabulary

four – 4	year n
nine – 9	dark adj
seven – 7	light adj
afternoon n	get up v
day n	go v
home n	is v
hour n	the det
minute n	o'clock adv
month n	for prep
morning n	in prep
night n	to prep
school n	it pron
time n	or conj
week n	what int

Follow-up work

Ask the children to draw a cartoon strip of the activities they do throughout a typical day, with pictures of clocks showing the time. Invite individuals to present their work to the class, saying the times and describing the activities they have recorded, eg

It's ten to eight in the morning. I have breakfast and clean my teeth.
It's midday. I have lunch.

The children could also design a diary for one week, writing what they do on each day of the week and at what time. If they have learnt the names of school subjects, these can be included as well as leisure activities. Invite individuals to present their diaries to the class, eg

On Wednesday at half past four I go swimming.

What time is it?

What time is it? Is it day or night?
What's the time? Is it dark or light?
It's seven o'clock in the morning,
Tick tock tick tock,
It's seven o'clock, it's time to get up.

Second, minute, hour, day, week, month, year.
Second, minute, hour, day, week, month, year.
Week, month, year, week, month, year!

What time is it? Is it day or night?
What's the time? Is it dark or light?
It's nine o'clock in the morning,
Tick tock tick tock,
It's nine o'clock, it's time for school.

Second, minute, hour, day, week, month, year ...

What time is it? Is it day or night?
What's the time? Is it dark or light?
It's four o'clock in the afternoon,
Tick tock tick tock,
It's four o'clock, it's time to go home.

Second, minute, hour, day, week,
month, year ...

Tick tock tick tock tick tock,
Time!

At school

audio tracks **33** the song **34** backing track

Using the song

First teach the class the names of the school subjects listed in the chorus. Make sure the children know that PE stands for physical education. Listen to the song (track 33) and join in with the chorus.

Teach the phrases in the verses. All sing the whole song, first with track 33 and then with the backing track (track 34).

A confident individual may sing the verses as a solo, with the whole class singing the chorus.

Developing the vocabulary

Introduce additional vocabulary for classroom objects, eg

calculator	eraser	pencil
computer	felt-tip	pencil
case crayon	glue	ruler
dictionary	paper	scissors

As a class, make up new lines for the verses using the new vocabulary, eg

Where are your crayons, paper and pen?
Fetch some scissors and some glue.

All sing the new version of the song with the backing track (track 34). Introduce

the names of other school subjects, eg

citizenship	**DT** (design and technology)
drama	**ICT** (information and
French	communication technology)
German	**PSHE** (personal, social and
Spanish	health education)
	RE (religious education)

art n	open v
book n	pick up v
English n	put v
geography n	shout v
hand n	sit down v
history n	try v
maths n	your det
music n	again adv
pen n	just adv
science n	out adv
work n	outside adv
good adj	up adv
don't v	well adv
go v	and conj
have v	

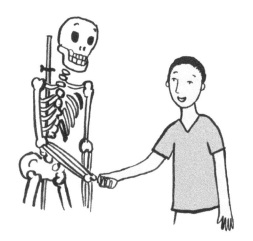

Follow-up work

Select a classroom object and show it to the class, asking **What is this?** The class or an individual responds by identifying the object, eg **It's a felt-tip.**

When the children have been introduced to the vocabulary for colours, they may add the appropriate colour, eg **It's a red felt-tip.**

As a class, prepare a large timetable showing the days Monday to Friday and the lessons the class has each day. Display the timetable on the classroom wall. Each morning, invite an individual to introduce the day's lessons, eg

It's Monday today. This morning we have English and maths. After lunch we have PE, then art.

At school

Sit down. Books out.
Put up your hand. Don't shout!
Sit down. Books out.
Put up your hand. Don't shout!
Open your book. Pick up your pen.
Don't give up. Try again!
Open your book. Pick up your pen.
Don't give up, just try again!

English, maths, history,
Geography, technology,
Art, music, science and PE.
English, maths, history,
Geography, technology,
Art, music, science and PE.

Good work. Well done.
Go outside. Have fun!
Good work. Well done.
Go outside. Have fun!

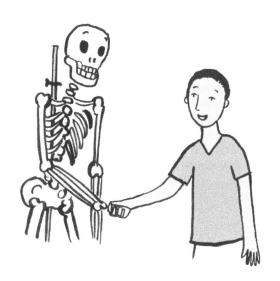

photocopiable

What do you want to be?

audio tracks   **35** the song   **36** backing track

Using the song

Listen to the song (track 35). Explain any new vocabulary in the rapped verses, then all join in with the verses as they become familiar.

Teach the chorus either by listening to the song or by saying the words yourself for the children to copy. Ensure that the children understand the occupations mentioned in the last two lines of the chorus.

Point out that **an** is used instead of **a** before nouns beginning with a vowel, eg **an actor**, **an artist**. Also check that the children are familiar with the short forms **you're (you are)** and **I'll (I shall/will)**.

When everyone is confident, perform the whole song with the backing track (track 36). If you wish, you can allocate two small groups one verse each, while the rest of the class sings the chorus.

Developing the vocabulary

Introduce more vocabulary for occupations and places of work, eg

businessman/woman	secretary	office
doctor	nurse	hospital
firefighter		fire station
mechanic		garage
pilot		airport
policeman/woman		police station

In pairs, the children compose new verses of the song with their own choice of occupations, eg

I want to be a mechanic, mechanic, mechanic, I'll fix cars in a garage ...

Invite pairs to perform their verses with the backing track (track 36), while the rest of the class sings the chorus.

key vocabulary

actor n	do v
artist n	is v
child/children n	teach v
dentist n	want v
farmer n	work v
food n	a det
footballer n	an det
restaurant n	the det
school n	in prep
singer n	I pron
teacher n	that pron
old adj	you pron
are v	when conj
be v	or conj
cook v	what int

Follow-up work

Play **What's my job?** Choose an occupation and invite the children to ask you questions to find out what your job is. The questions may only be answered **yes** or **no**, eg

Do you work in an office?	No
Do you work outside?	Yes
Do you work with animals?	Yes
Are you a farmer?	Yes

If the children have difficulty working out the occupation, give them a clue by miming the job.

The child who correctly identifies the occupation may choose another occupation and ask **What's my job?** to start the game again.

What do you want to be?

When you're older, when you're grown up,
What do you want to do?
When you're older, when you're grown up,
What do you want to be?
An actor, an artist, a singer in a band,

A footballer, a dentist or a farmer who works the land?

I want to be a teacher, a teacher, a teacher,
I'll teach children in a school.
I want to be a teacher, a teacher, a teacher,
That's what I want to be.

When you're older, when you're
grown up ...

I want to be a chef, a chef, a chef,
I'll cook food in a restaurant.
I want to be a chef, a chef, a chef,
That's what I want to be.

Which way?

Using the song

Begin by teaching the class the directions in the song and their meanings:

Go left   **Go straight ahead**
Turn right   **Cross the road**

Listen to the song (track 37). Explain the other new vocabulary in the chorus. Then listen to the song again and all join in with the chorus.

Teach the verses either by listening to the song or by saying the words yourself for the children to copy. Make sure the children know the meaning of the words.

Sing the whole song with track 37, then with the backing track (track 38).

Developing the vocabulary

Introduce the names of more places, eg

bank	**cinema**	**police station**
bus station	**library**	**post office**
café	**market**	**swimming pool**

Invite the class to choose three new place names to use in the song. You could also compose a new chorus, eg

Turn right, go straight ahead,
Take the second road on the left,
Then cross the road at the traffic lights,
And there you are!

Sing the new version of the song with the backing track (track 38).

In pairs, the children prepare new versions of the song with their own choice of places and directions. Divide the class into two groups to perform some of the ideas with the backing track, taking it in turns to ask for and give directions.

Afterwards, three pairs may like to perform a new version of the song to the class, each pair taking a turn to sing their own verse and chorus.

key vocabulary

bookshop n	far adv
bridge n	left adv
bus stop n	not adv
light n	right adv
road n	then adv
station n	very adv
traffic n	straight ahead adv
way n	
can v	at prep
cross v	to prep
go v	under prep
help v	it pron
is v	me pron
tell v	you pron
turn v	which int
the det	excuse me inter
	please inter

Follow-up work

Play **Map reader**. Draw a simple map of a town, showing roads and labelling some buildings, eg **bank**, **post office**. Display the map where all the children can see it.

Mark a starting point on the map and select a child to come to the front and choose a destination. The child then asks the class for directions, eg

Which is the way to the cinema, please?

Invite individuals to offer directions one at a time, eg

Go straight ahead.
Turn left at the café.

The child follows the route on the map with a finger or with a pen as the directions are given.

Repeat the game, giving other children the opportunity to ask for directions.

Which way?

Excuse me, can you help me?
Which is the way to the station?
Excuse me, can you tell me?
Which is the way to the station, please?

Go left, turn right,
Go straight ahead, under the bridge,
Then cross the road at the traffic lights,
It's not very far!

Excuse me, can you help me?
Which is the way to the bus stop?
Excuse me, can you tell me?
Which is the way to the bus stop, please?

Go left, turn right ...

Excuse me, can you help me?
Which is the way to the bookshop?
Excuse me, can you tell me?
Which is the way to the bookshop, please?

Go left, turn right ...

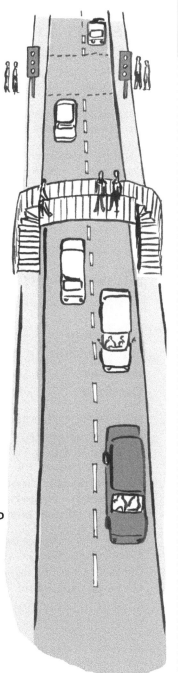

SINGING ENGLISH © HELEN MACGREGOR & STEPHEN CHADWICK 2005, HarperCollins*Publishers* Ltd

On holiday

audio tracks **39** the song **40** backing track

Using the song

Listen to the song (track 39), then teach the class the chorus either using the song or by saying the words yourself for the children to copy. You may wish to point out the countries on a map or globe.

Listen to the song again, all joining in with the line **Have a great time on holiday!** each time it is sung.

Teach the class the verses. You could use actions to help the children memorise the activities (**swimming, climbing, skiing, seeing the pyramids**).

When everyone is familiar with the vocabulary, perform the whole song with track 39, then with the backing track (track 40).

Developing the vocabulary

Teach the class the names of other countries, eg

Australia	**Greece**	**New Zealand**
Bangladesh	**Japan**	**Pakistan**
Belgium	**Morocco**	**Russia**
Canada	**the Netherlands**	**Turkey**

As a class, choose four new holiday destinations and compose new verses, eg

I'm going to the Netherlands
To ride a bike.
Have a great time on holiday!
I'm going to Canada
To watch the whales.
Have a great time on holiday!

Sing the new version of the song with the backing track (track 40). You could select four confident individuals to sing the verses. The whole class sings the chorus and the England verse, as well as the line **Have a great time on holiday!** each time it occurs.

key vocabulary

holiday n	see v
mountain n	ski v
pyramid n	swim v
sea n	a det
time n	the det
am v	in prep
are v	on prep
climb v	to prep
go v	I pron
have v	it pron
learn v	you pron
rain v	where int

Follow-up work

Collect posters, leaflets and travel brochures from travel agents', tourist information centres or the internet. Include places to visit in the UK as well as other countries.

Encourage the children to investigate different places and to decide where they would like to go on holiday. Do a survey and draw a class bar chart to show the most popular destinations.

Set up a travel agency for children to role play questions and answers. Encourage them to incorporate transport vocabulary, eg

Customer: **I'd like to go to Belfast. How do I get there?**

Travel agent: **You can travel by plane or by boat. It's quicker by plane!**

On holiday

France, Spain, Germany, Italy,
Scotland, Ireland, England, Wales,
China, the USA, Africa, India,
Where are you going on holiday?

I'm going to the seaside
To swim in the sea.
Have a great time on holiday!
I'm going to Scotland
To climb the mountains.
Have a great time on holiday!

France, Spain, Germany, Italy ...

I'm going to the Alps
To learn to ski.
Have a great time on holiday!
I'm going to Egypt
To see the pyramids.
Have a great time on holiday!

France, Spain, Germany, Italy ...

I'm going to England,
I hope it doesn't rain.
Have a great time on holiday!

In my dreams

the world around us

audio tracks   **41** the song   **42** backing track

Using the song

Listen to the song (track 41), all joining in with the chorus as it becomes familiar.

Teach the verses one at a time, either by listening to the song or by saying the words yourself for the children to copy. Ensure that the children understand the meaning of the words.

When everyone is confident with the vocabulary, divide the class into two groups and practise singing the end of verse 3 in two parts. Perform the song with track 41, then with the backing track (track 42).

Developing the vocabulary

Teach the class more vocabulary relating to the world around us, eg

cave	lake	river
island	moon	star
jungle	mountain	village

Also introduce useful adjectives for describing environments, eg

cold/hot	high/low
dark/light	noisy/quiet
dry/wet	

Play **Where am I?** Write a list of environments on the board, eg **cave, city, countryside, island, jungle, mountain, sea, space**. Choose an environment and invite the children to ask you three questions which may only be answered **yes, no** or **sometimes**. Once the three questions have been asked, invite them to guess where you are, eg

Is it noisy?	Answer: **No**
Is it cold?	Answer: **Yes**
Is it dark?	Answer: **Yes**
Are you in a cave?	Answer: **Yes/No, I am in space.**

When the children are familiar with the game, encourage small groups to play, taking it in turns to ask questions. Ensure that each child has a turn at choosing an environment.

city n	am v
country(side) n	go v
cow n	is v
field n	look v
forest n	meet v
goat n	see v
horse n	a det
person/people n	many det
place n	my det
planet n	the det
sheep (s + pl) n	this det
space n	away adv
street n	far adv
town n	here adv
traffic n	out adv
beautiful adj	there adv
brown adj	in prep
gold adj	from prep
green adj	on prep
quiet adj	everyone pron
strange adj	I pron
yellow adj	it pron
	and conj

Follow-up work

Collect travel agents' brochures with pictures of different environments, such as beaches, cities, mountains, jungles and rivers. In small groups, the children choose an environment and make a travel poster with pictures and captions. They could carry out further research using geography books, maps or the internet.

When the groups have completed their posters, invite them to show and describe them to the class, eg

On this island there are beautiful beaches. The sun is shining and the sea is blue.

In my dreams

In the city, I see buildings and streets,
Many people, it's where everyone meets.
Busy traffic all around,
In the city. (Ah)

In my dreams, in my dreams,
I go there
In my dreams. (Ah)

In the country, far away from the town,
Fields and forests, yellow, green, gold and brown.
Cows and horses, sheep and goats,
In the country. (Ah)

In my dreams, in my dreams ...

On a planet, far away out in space,
I'm alone here in this strange, quiet place
And the Earth looks beautiful
From this planet,

☺ **From this planet,** ☺ **In my dreams, in my**
From this planet,   **dreams, I go there**
From this planet.   **In my dreams.**
(Ah, ah)   **(Ah, ah)**

Washday blues

Using the song

Listen to the song (track 43) and all join in with the last line of each verse as it becomes familiar (**Around and around in the washing machine**). Listen to the song again and teach the chorus of verses two, three and four (**Hubble bubble ...**), either using the song or by saying the words yourself for the children to copy.

Then teach verse one and the lines which describe the items of clothing. Ensure that the children understand the meaning of the vocabulary.

Sing the whole song with track 43, then with the backing track (track 44). The children may wish to devise actions or a dance to perform as they sing.

Developing the vocabulary

Introduce the class to more vocabulary for items of clothing, eg

belt	**jumper**
cap	**tights/pair of tights**
hat	**trainers/pair of trainers**
jacket	**trousers/pair of trousers**

Also introduce other adjectives to describe clothing, eg

black	**orange**	**favourite**
blue	**pink**	**horrible**
brown	**red**	**long**
gold	**silver**	**lovely**
green	**white**	**pretty**
grey	**expensive**	**short**

Ask small groups or pairs to use this vocabulary to create a new verse for the song, eg

A pair of trousers, my favourite cap,
A lovely coat, a horrible hat!

All perform some of the new verses with the backing track (track 44).

key vocabulary

clothes n	get v
coat n	have v
dress n	is v
glove n	look v
jeans n	put on v
scarf n	will v
shirt n	a det
shoe n	all det
shorts n	my det
skirt n	some det
sock n	the det
sweater n	those det
time n	just adv
T-shirt n	much adv
winter n	today adv
better adj	in prep
clean adj	anything pron
dirty adj	I pron
purple adj	it pron
yellow adj	they pron
are v	and conj
can't v	when conj
find v	where int

Follow-up work

Teach the class the phrases **I am wearing** and **he/she is wearing**.

Hold a class fashion show. Select children to model items of clothing and a presenter to describe to the class what is being worn, eg

Karl is wearing long green trousers and a black and white shirt.

Allow children to take turns to do the presenting.

Ask the children to cut out pictures of famous people from magazines and to describe what they are wearing. Their appearance can also be described once the appropriate vocabulary has been learnt, eg

His name is David Beckham. He has short, fair hair. He is wearing a red T-shirt, stripy shorts and expensive trainers.

Washday blues

Today I've got those washday blues,
Dirty T-shirts, socks and shoes,
Where have all my clean clothes gone?
I just can't find anything to put on!
It's time to get my washing clean,
Around and around in the washing machine.

Some denim jeans, a yellow dress,
Some dirty shorts, what a mess!
Hubble bubble, hubble bubble, rinse and spin.
Hubble bubble, hubble bubble, rinse and spin.
It's time to get my washing clean,
Around and around in the washing machine.

A pair of gloves, a purple shirt,
A stripy scarf, a spotted skirt.
Hubble bubble, hubble bubble, rinse and spin …

A winter coat, a woollen sweater,
When they're clean they'll look much better.
Hubble bubble, hubble bubble, rinse and spin …

The washing machine!
The washing machine!

Melody lines

1 Hello (p6)

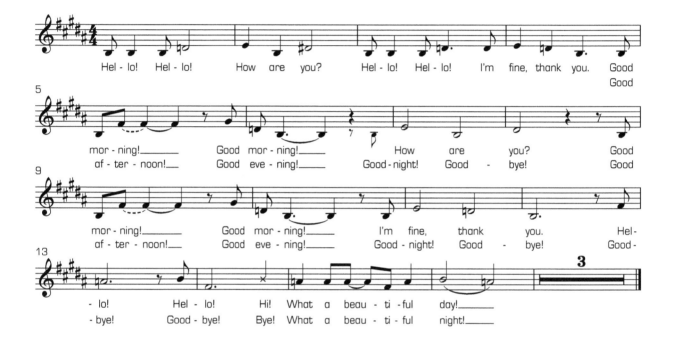

3 The human body (p8)

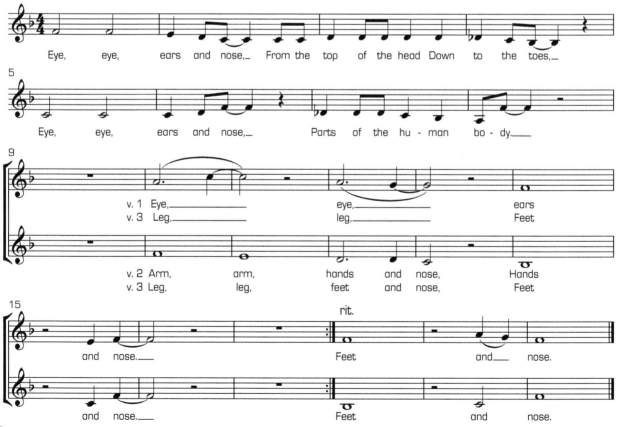

5 One to ten and back again (p10)

Get rea - dy! Count to ten, Up to ten, then back a - gain.

One two three four five, One two three four five,
Ten nine eight se - ven six, Ten nine eight se - ven six,

Six se - ven eight nine ten. Six se - ven eight nine ten.
Five four three two one. Five four three two one.

One two three four five six se - ven Eight nine ten.
Ten nine eight se - ven six five four Three two one.

One two three four five six se - ven Eight nine ten. Get
Ten nine eight se - ven six five four Three two

one. Count up high, count down low, And don't for - get

ze - ro! (Ze - ro! Ze - ro! Ze - ro! Ze - ro! Ze - ro!)

7 My favourite food (p12)

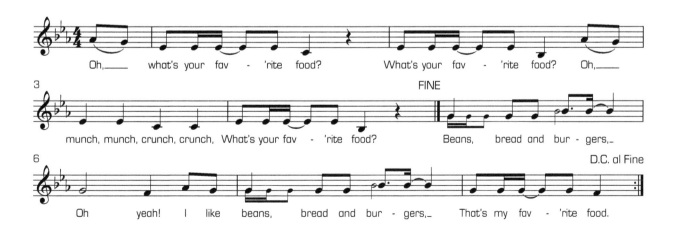

Oh,____ what's your fav - 'rite food? What's your fav - 'rite food? Oh,____

munch, munch, crunch, crunch, What's your fav - 'rite food? Beans, bread and bur - gers,_

Oh yeah! I like beans, bread and bur - gers,_ That's my fav - 'rite food.

Melody lines

9 The alphabet (p14)

Say the al-pha-bet with me, A B C D Keep to the beat and you will see,

A B C D E F G Learn-ing the al-pha-bet is

ea - sy! A B C D E F G H I

J K L M N O P Stay cool and use your head, You start at A and

end at Z! A B C D E F G H I J K

L M N O P Q R S T U V W_____ X Y Z

11 I like swimming (p16)

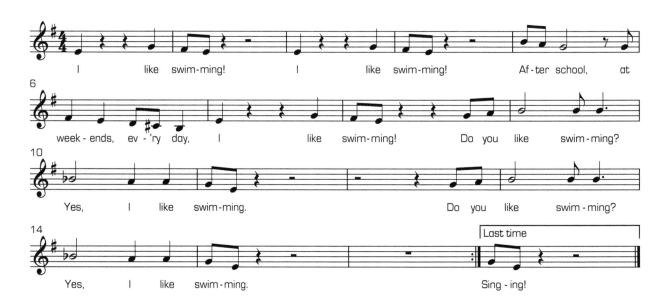

I like swim-ming! I like swim-ming! Af-ter school, at

week - ends, ev-'ry day, I like swim-ming! Do you like swim-ming?

Yes, I like swim-ming. Do you like swim-ming?

Last time

Yes, I like swim-ming. Sing-ing!

13 My family (p18)

I'd like you to meet all my fa-mi-ly,
Fa-ther, mo-ther,
Aunt, un-cle,

sis-ter, bro-ther, Meet my fa-mi-ly,___ meet my fa-mi-ly.___
grand-pa-rents,

These are my pa-rents, Mum and Dad,___ This is my sis-ter___
This is my Aun-ty___ E-mi-ly, This is my Un-cle___

Ka-tie,___ This is my ba-by bro-ther, Da-vid,
Mi-chael,___ This is my Grand-ma and my Gran-dad,

This is my fa-mi-ly,___ this is my fa-mi-ly.___

Now you've said 'How do you do?'___ to my fa-mi-ly, Come in-side___ and make your-

-self at home! Let's all have some tea!

Let's all have some tea!

Melody lines

15 My house (p20)

When you come to stay__ with me, We will have a par - ty! All my friends will be__

6

__ there too, When you stay at my__ house. There's a goat in the gar - den.__

12 |2.|

cro - co - dile in the kit - chen__ And a goat in the gar - den.__

17 |3.|

liz - ard in the liv - ing room, a cro - co - dile in the kit - chen And a goat in the gar - den.__

24 |4.|

bat in the bath - room,__ a liz - ard in the liv - ing room,__ a

28

cro - co - dile in the kit - chen__ And a goat in the gar - den.__

33

All my friends are in the house, All my friends are in the house!

17 Ten to one hundred (p22)

Ten, e - le - ven, twelve, thir - teen, Four - teen, fif - teen.

Six - teen, se - ven - teen,___ Eigh - teen, nine - teen, twen - ty. Car - ry on in tens,

Twen - ty, thir - ty, for - ty, fif - ty. Six - ty, se - ven - ty,___ Eigh - ty,

nine - ty, one hun - dred. Ten to one hun - dred. Ten to one hun - dred.

19 Are you hungry? (p24)

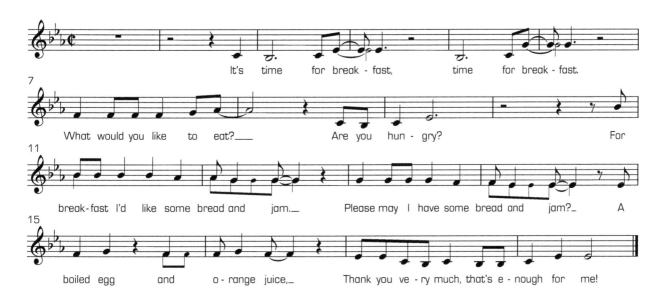

It's time for break - fast, time for break - fast.

What would you like to eat?___ Are you hun - gry? For

break - fast I'd like some bread and jam.___ Please may I have some bread and jam?_ A

boiled egg and o - range juice,_ Thank you ve - ry much, that's e - nough for me!

Melody lines

21 **Everyone is travelling** (p26)

Tra - vel - ling,__ tra - vel - ling,__ Tra - vel - ling,__ oh yeah! Ev - 'ry - one is tra - vel - ling

All o - ver the world. Tra - vel - ling,__ tra - vel - ling,__ Tra - vel - ling,__ oh yeah!

How will we get__ there?__ All o - ver the world. We can tra - vel in a car,

Tra - vel on a train, On a bus, on a boat, Or in a plane. But the

best way to tra - vel, If it is - n't too far,__ Is to put on your shoes__ And

walk, walk, walk, walk, Put on your shoes and walk, walk, walk.

23 **Weather report** (p28)

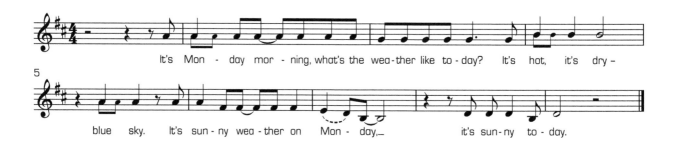

It's Mon - day mor - ning, what's the wea - ther like to - day? It's hot, it's dry –

blue sky. It's sun - ny wea - ther on Mon - day,__ it's sun - ny to - day.

25 People all over the world (p30)

27 Going shopping (p32)

Melody lines

29 Happy birthday (p34)

31 What time is it? (p36)

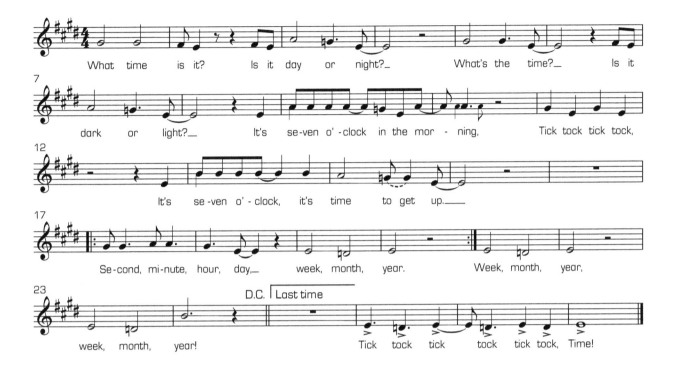

What time is it? Is it day or night?— What's the time?— Is it
dark or light?— It's se-ven o'-clock in the mor - ning, Tick tock tick tock,
It's se -ven o'-clock, it's time to get up.——
Se-cond, mi-nute, hour, day,— week, month, year. Week, month, year,

D.C. | Last time
week, month, year! Tick tock tick tock tick tock, Time!

33 At school (p38)

Sit down. Books out. Put up your hand. Don't shout! Sit down. Books out. Put up your
hand. Don't shout! O-pen your book. Pick up your pen. Don't give up.
Try a - gain! O-pen your book. Pick up your pen. Don't give up, just try a -
-gain! Eng-lish, maths, his-to-ry,— Ge-og-ra-phy, tech-no-lo-gy,——
Art, mu-sic, sci-ence and P - E.—— Good work. Well done.
Go out-side. Have fun! Good work. Well done. Go out-side. Have fun!

Melody lines

35 What do you want to be? (p40)

When you're old - er, when you're grown up, What do you want to do?___

When you're old - er, when you're grown up, What do you want to be?___ An

ac - tor, an ar - tist, a sing - er in a band,___ A

foot - ball - er, a den - tist or a far - mer who works the land?___ I want to be a

teach - er, a teach - er, a teach - er, I'll teach child - ren in a school.___ I want to be a

teach - er, a teach - er, a teach - er, That's what I want to be.___

37 Which way? (p42)

Ex - cuse me, can you help me? Which is the way to the sta - tion? Ex -

- cuse me, can you tell me? Which is the way to the sta - tion, please? Go left, turn right, Go

straight a - head,___ un - der the bridge, Then cross the road___ at the traf - fic lights, It's

1.2.

not ve - ry far!___

3.

Ex - not ve - ry far!___

39 On holiday [p44]

France, Spain, Ger-ma-ny, I-ta-ly, Scot-land, Ire-land, Eng-land, Wales,

3rd time to Coda

Chi-na, the U-S-A, Af-ri-ca, In-di-a, Where are you go-ing on ho-li-day? I'm
I'm
I'm

go-ing to the sea-side To swim in the sea. Have a great time___ on
go-ing to the Alps To learn to ski.

hol-i-day! I'm go-ing to Scot-land To climb the moun-tains.
I'm go-ing to E-gypt To see the py-ra-mids.

CODA
Slowly

Have a great time___ on ho-li-day!

go-ing to Eng-land, I

hope it does-n't rain. Have a great time___ on ho-li-day!

Melody lines

41 In my dreams (p46)

43 Washday blues (p48)

Swung ♩♩ = ♩ ³ ♪

To - day I've got those wash-day blues, Dir - ty T - shirts,

socks and shoes, Where have all my clean clothes gone?_ I just can't find a - ny-

-thing to put on!_ It's time to get my wash-ing clean,_ A - round and a - round in the

wash-ing ma - chine._____ Some de - nim jeans, a

yel-low dress, Some dir - ty shorts, what a mess! Hub-ble bub-ble, hub-ble bub-ble,

rinse and spin._ Hub-ble bub-ble, hub-ble bub-ble, rinse and spin._ It's time to get my wash-ing clean,_

1.2.

_ A - round and a - round in the wash-ing ma - chine._____ A

3.

_ The wash-ing ma - chine!_____ The wash-ing ma - chine!_____

Track list

Track Contents

Acknowledgements

The authors and publishers would like to thank the following people for their help in the preparation of this resource:
Kath Appleton, Susan Balis, Catherine Bolland, Jude Brennan, Kim Chandler, Robert Foss, Jean-Pierre Giraud, Oscar Heini, Adelheid Kramer, Paul Langridge, Harriet Lowe, Jocelyn Lucas, Chris Madin, Asha Pandit, Marie Penny, Lucy Poddington, Cath Rasbash, Silke Redetzki, Jeanne Roberts, Tricia Scott, David Shanks, Fran Warden and Emily Wilson.

www.ingramcontent.com/pod-product-compliance
Ingram Content Group UK Ltd.
Pitfield, Milton Keynes, MK11 3LW, UK
UKHW050104260325
456708UK00012BA/165